THE SECRET POWER OF A CAUSE

TURNING DREAMS INTO MIRACLES

PASTOR BOB NICHOLS

THE SECRET POWER OF A CAUSE

TURNING DREAMS INTO MIRACLES

BY PASTOR BOB NICHOLS

Compassion House Publishing | Fort Worth, Texas

ISBN 0-9754200-1-1

Unless otherwise indicated, all Scripture quotations are taken from the *King James Version* of the Bible.

The Secret Power of a Cause
ISBN. 0-9754200-1-90000
Copyright 2004 by Calvary Cathedral, Inc.
1701 Oakhurst Scenic Drive
Fort Worth, Texas 76111

Printed in the United States of America. All rights reserved under International Copyright Law. Contents and/or cover may not be reproduced in whole or in part in any form without the expressed written consent of the publisher.

Contents

Foreword ii

Acknowledgments iv

1 / From Vision To Cause 11

2 / I Can Do No Other 15

3 / The Unstoppable Cause 23

4 / Is There Not A Cause? 31

5 / To This End Was I Born 37

6 / What's In It For Me? 41

7 / Pursuing Your Cause 47

Acknowledgments

I would like to say thank you to Glenn Tidwell, Mark Carrillo, and Renae Cockroft. I appreciate your many hours of diligent work. I am so grateful for your partnership in seeing this project completed. The subject of this book is a passionate one for me and I am thankful to you for helping me to express it.

Foreword

"Is there not a cause?" David's question to his brothers immediately created an atmosphere for a spiritual showdown of great proportions between the God of Israel and the god of the Philistine. A statement of this magnitude left no room for retreat. My country, Uganda, was declared to be a moslem country by the dictator Idi Amin. After this declaration, there was an atmosphere of death. But when God spoke to Papa Bob Nichols about helping to build a Christian television station in Uganda, a new atmosphere was created. Lighthouse Television is now preaching the gospel, 24 hours a day, 7 days a week in Uganda, Africa.

Recently, in a gathering to celebrate Uganda's independence, His Excellency President Museveni said, "I always watch Lighthouse Television." The television station is making a difference in our country. On behalf of my country and all Christians in Uganda, we are grateful to Papa Bob Nichols for being obedient to the Holy Spirit to come all the way from Fort Worth, Texas, USA to bring us the gift of the Gospel of Jesus Christ that sets the captives free. Why does Papa Bob Nichols fight for souls in Africa even after his own church building was destroyed by a tornado? It is because he knows there is a cause. It is not about us; it is about God's will on the earth. We must fight for our nations and our generations. Is there not a cause that will stir your passion to see God's will accomplished and bring forth victory for all?

Pastor Robert Kayanja
Miracle Centre Cathedral, Kampala, Uganda

Chapter 1

FROM VISION TO CAUSE

*"Where there is no vision,
the people perish."*
Proverbs 29:18

Thousands of framed vision statements hang on the walls of companies all over the world. It is a trendy thing to do in our modern society. These vision statements are the products of eager, optimistic people who work hard to convey to employees and to the public what the company intends to do or to be in the future. But for every vision statement that is hung in the lobby of a successful business, there are many vision statements that are written but will never be achieved. Somewhere along the way, regardless of how good the vision may sound, it is shelved. Perhaps the cost of achieving the vision is underestimated, or maybe too much work is involved, or possibly the excitement that was evident in the beginning cannot be maintained.

Unfortunately, businesses are not the only ones that sometimes abandon the original vision. Many Christians allow the vision to fade or disappear as well. In order to understand how a God-given vision can be forgotten, we need to explore the limitations of a vision.

What exactly is a vision? A vision is a compass providing steady guidance along the path that God is leading you. It is a divine point of reference that steadies you and keeps your eyes off of present circumstances and allows you to see the prize ahead of you. When difficulties arise, the

> *The vision is vitally important to the believer, but it does not guarantee success.*

vision reminds you of your future success. The Bible has many things to say about the importance of a vision. Proverbs 29:18 says, *"Where there is no vision, the people perish."* Without a vision, there is no sense of direction. The vision is vitally important to the believer, but it does not guarantee success. The problem with a vision is that it can be put on the shelf or forgotten altogether. A vision is optional. If the glamorous vision becomes too difficult to achieve, it can easily be put aside. A vision is needed, but there is something more.

In Acts chapter 26, Paul is testifying before King

Agrippa about his encounter with Jesus. He tells the king about how Jesus changed his life and how he knew he had to accomplish what God wanted him to do. A vision was birthed in his heart on the road to Damascus. In verse 19 of chapter 26, Paul tells the king that he had *"not been disobedient to the heavenly vision."* Paul kept the vision before him. He knew his duty was to spread the good news and his vision kept him on track. His vision provided a reference point that encouraged him to continue *"pressing toward the mark for the prize of the high calling in Christ Jesus."* (Philippians 3:14). Paul was given a vision on the road to Damascus, but somewhere along the way there was a shift that took place. He knew his vision would not come to pass unless he went to work. The vision that God gave to Paul on the road to Damascus became a passionate cause. **His vision became a cause.**

Chapter 2

I Can Do No Other

*"Thus saith the LORD,
the Holy One of Israel, and his Maker,
'Ask me of things to come concerning my sons,
and concerning the work of my hands
command ye me.'"*
Isaiah 45:11

When I was a young man I was a rebel without a cause. My parents were godly people who prayed for me and simply would not let the devil have me. My mother poured herself into my life and gave me a solid foundation in the Word of God. I ran from God's plan for a period of time as a teenager, but my mother and God refused to let me go to hell. I remember coming home on many occasions late at night hoping to sneak to my bed, and I would hear my mother purposely praying for me loud enough for me to hear. She knew that God had a plan for me.

Although I was running from God, He had a way of

getting my attention from time to time. On one particular occasion, Oral Roberts came to our town and pitched his gospel tent in the parking lot of a local football stadium. One night, I decided to attend one of the tent meetings with some friends of mine. God was changing lives under the tent and many people came to the Lord that night. It moved me. I remember turning to my friends and saying, "Someday I will preach the gospel of Jesus Christ." I had never said that in my life up to that point. It was a word that came from the Spirit of God. Of course my friends just laughed and shrugged it off, but I know that I heard the call of God that night. I didn't try to defend it; it just came right out of my spirit. On that night I knew that God had called me into the ministry. I will always be grateful to Oral Roberts for coming to Fort Worth.

    Some years later, after attending bible college, I began serving as an associate minister in my father-in-law's church. I served faithfully for eight years learning how to minister to people. But when God opened the door for us to plant our church, we knew we had to seize the moment. The vision that God had birthed in my heart, years before, suddenly became a cause. It was time. The God-opportunity presented itself and we seized it. It was no longer a future vision in my mind. It was real.

    We had no people or finances so we leased an old post office building with an option to purchase. This gave us a place that we could call home. We had much remodeling to do. I was the pastor, the music minister, the janitor, the contractor, and many other things. I even had to learn to operate a jackhammer to break up concrete floors in the remodeling process. They did not teach us how to handle a jackhammer in bible college. All of a sudden, this great vision became hard work. Why did I do it? I did it because it was my passion. I wanted to see souls saved and people helped. I believed that our little building was going to be used by God. This cause consumed me. It was why I was born. It was the point of no return. God had given us the opportunity because the time was right. I welcomed it and have never looked back. My vision became a cause.

Then one day we got a call from the First Baptist Church in downtown Fort Worth, Texas. They were interested in selling their facility. They knew we were looking for a bigger place. It was definitely a bigger place! It seated 2,000! To me it felt like the difference between a bicycle and an eighteen-wheeler truck. I remembered that I had seen that auditorium before in 1964, while it was under construction. It was the biggest auditorium I had seen. I said, "I would give anything to see a building like this used to preach the whole gospel." It was overwhelming in the natural. But the more I prayed about it, the more excited I got. I began to think about how many lives God could touch and how many souls could be saved. My faith locked onto that building and I became determined that it would be ours. Many people told me that I could not make it.

Some people thought I was crazy. I had people walk out of board meetings and resign because they thought I was making a huge mistake.

But I had a word from God. God showed me in Isaiah 43 that just as He had been with Israel, He would also be with me. This became the scriptural foundation for this great step of faith. The original vision had become a cause. I knew that this cause was bigger than me and that I could put my trust in God and He would make a way.

The biggest hurdle was going to be finances. I began searching for a financial institution that would be willing to take a risk on a small church. In the natural, it did not look promising. I approached seemingly every financial institution and was turned down time after time. Many of these banks told me that they would not invest in churches. It was too risky. Of course, after forty years, some of those banks have changed their name five or six times, and we are still here. God had a plan. God honors faith.

> *A cause is total faith commitment.*

We tried everything. It seemed so impossible in the natural. But there was nothing I would not try as long as it was legal. There was nowhere I would not fly. There was nowhere I would not drive. Whatever it took, I was going to get the financing for the property. I remember one banker said to me, "Man, you act like you are possessed." I was possessed! If it had only been a vision, I would have quit. But I had a cause.

We were able to make the move into the new church initially by assuming the note that the previous church still had on the property. The only drawback was that the financing was temporary and there was also a significant balloon payment that would be coming due as well. We were going to have to find someone who was willing to extend the financing. We continued to be unsuccessful at getting a loan for a good length of time. Then one day, we received a notice stating that we were going to have to vacate the property within thirty days if we did not get the financing! It came down to thirty days.

Everything that we had worked for was in the balance and was dependent upon getting the money. Needless to say, I felt a tremendous amount of pressure. I remember driving in my car feeling an enormous weight on my shoulders. I was crying and praying. But it wasn't long before God reminded me of Isaiah 45:11 which says, *"Thus saith the LORD, the Holy One of Israel, and his Maker, 'Ask me of things to come concerning my sons, and concerning the work of my hands command ye me.'"* I was reminded through this scripture that because this was God's work, He would come through. He is always faithful to honor His Word. I locked into a radical faith born of the heart of God.

It was in God's hands and I knew somehow He would make a way.

Just a short time before our deadline, I met with representatives from the First Baptist Church and some bankers in order to try to acquire permanent financing. This would allow us to stay in the downtown property. I was not having much success. In fact, these men were really trying to discourage me. They were telling me that I was wasting their time and that I was never going to get the financing. I was ready to leave, but one man asked to see me in another room. He asked me to tell the story of the church one more time. He wanted to know our history, our vision, and our level of commitment. I really didn't even want to tell it again. I was frustrated but I decided to tell the story once more. I told him about how many broken-hearted people had been saved, helped and healed through our church, and how alcoholics and drug addicts had been delivered. I told him that I believed God had big plans for our growing church. Before I was finished, he was weeping and announced to me that he would personally make sure that we got the money that we needed! As it turned out, he was a back-slidden Baptist minister.

> *When you are passionate about a cause, nothing can deter you.*

He went back into the room where the others were and announced to everyone that he would get us the financing. In 90 days it was done. Praise God! God is truly faithful. When a vision turns into a cause, anything is possible.

The reason I tell you this story is because I want to illustrate how when you are passionate about a cause, nothing can deter you. A cause is total faith commitment. It is unstoppable. When you are consumed with a cause, nothing is too big or too small. Nothing is beneath your dignity. You will do whatever it takes to get the job done. The cause possesses the entirety of your being. Your vision graduates to a cause the moment you drive a stake in the ground and say, "Here I am, I can do no other." A vision is nice, but it will not get the job done. A vision is something *you possess; a cause possesses you*. The vision represents someday, the cause represents right now! Every person who has done great things for God has or had a cause. David embraced a cause, Paul had a cause and YOU have a cause. God wants to help you to fulfill your passionate cause. When the excitement of a vision has run its course, a cause will press on to victory.

Chapter 3

The Unstoppable Cause

"Beware lest any man spoil you through philosophy and vain deceit, after the tradition of men, after the rudiments of the world, and not after Christ."
Colossians 2:8

I am sold on the cause of Christian education. In fact, as a pastor of a local church for over 40 years, I believe that every church is called to either provide a Christian school or to actively support one. Christian education is critical to the future of Christianity in our nation and our world. It is needed now more than ever.

I have great respect and admiration for Christian teachers who are called to be in the mission fields of public education. But we have discovered that, in many cases, the support of Christian education has had to become a missions project as well. There is an all out attack of the enemy on this generation of Christian young people. Christian young people need to be in a godly, nurturing environment in order to grow and mature. We cannot leave them at the mercy of our godless society and expect them to come out okay.

What students are being taught in secular education concerns me greatly, but I am even more concerned about what they are not being taught. Christian education is about training up students to uphold godly standards in a dark world. A Christian school is not a perfect environment, but it is one that, at the very least, is not hostile to the Word of God. The name of Jesus can still be spoken boldly. Prayer is an important part of the school day. In our school, there are life changing chapels conducted weekly. The Bible is taught as the supreme authority. The 10 Commandments are still on our walls and in our teaching. Of course we are not saved by the 10 Commandments, but they are still the foundation of our society. We are saved by grace but the 10 Commandments teach us the fear of God and how to live life. We must provide young people with the proper envi-

> *We cannot be guilty of educating our children's minds at the expense of their souls.*

ronment to receive a true education—spirit, soul, and body. We cannot be guilty of educating our children's minds at the expense of their souls. God forbid!

In 1979, at the suggestion of some of the people in our congregation, our church decided to start a Christian school. It was a God idea. The vision was birthed in our hearts. We would provide a great school where kids from our church and others could get a solid academic education and more importantly, a solid biblical foundation. I felt a release from God to go for it. What a great vision! Young people would graduate from our school with the sharpest minds in the world and be sold out to God all at the same time! Why wouldn't we want to do that? It sounded so exciting! So we opened our humble little school with a great big vision.

It didn't take long before we realized that this vision would take some serious work and cost a lot of money. We made some mistakes in the beginning. No one told us that we should build our school by adding one grade at a time. Instead, we opened up our doors the first year serving kindergarten through 12th grade.

In the beginning years of our Christian school we learned some serious lessons. Christian education was not a glamorous endeavor. It was hard work. We were and still are privileged to do it, but it requires serious commitment. The reality of what we were endeavoring to do settled in. Suddenly, little children with dirty hands had invaded our beautiful building. There was wear and tear on the building that we had not had before. The utility expenses began to rise. We discovered that Christian education was more costly than we anticipated. Tuition alone was not going to cover all of the expenses. The reason our church has invested heavily into Calvary Christian Academy over the years is because it is a missions outreach. It is more than a vision; it is a cause.

As our school began to grow steadily, our expenses and pressures also began to grow, but we were beginning to see the fruit of our labor. Before long we were at our capacity. We did not have any room to grow as far as enrollment was concerned, but God was helping us to grow in excellence. But we did not realize the challenges that we would face in the near future.

On March 28, 2000, at around 6:30 in the evening, a tornado ripped through our building and in about 42 seconds, we lost everything. The church building was destroyed and our school wing was destroyed. The building was condemned within hours after the tornado struck. It was a miracle of God that no one was killed. I am so thankful that the school day had already ended and that most of the children were out of the building.

Our school year was coming to a close. Our graduation ceremony was scheduled to take place in a few short weeks. All of a sudden, we had no place for our school to meet. We were serving about 400 students a day in our

Christian school. At the time, everything seemed up in the air. Our teachers and support staff wondered if they would have jobs. Our students wondered if they would have a school. Where would all of our seniors graduate? Just a few days after the tornado I was so blessed to see a group of our high school students gathered at the site of the destroyed building to pray for the future of the school and church. We had nowhere to go but God was in control. We had embraced His cause and He had given us a passion to see it continue.

If I had been looking for an excuse to get out of Christian education, this would have been the perfect time. No one would have blamed me. After all, we no longer even had a building. We could have just closed up right then and there. But I can tell you right now, we were not going to give up. We had a cause. Quitting was not an option.

We began to search desperately for a place to finish out our school year. At the same time I was trying to find a place for our church to meet as well. It was a trying time, but I had a word from God. God had told me that we were going to come out with twice as much, just as Job had come out with twice as much in the Old Testament. We looked at several run-down buildings and found nothing that could facilitate a school of our size. But God had a plan.

About two weeks after the tornado, I received a phone call from the senior minister of Midtown Church of Christ church in Fort Worth. He offered to let us use their church building, just 3 miles from our former location, to house our school. I wasn't really sure if he knew what he was getting himself into but I agreed to talk to him and his church elders about it. We met and the board voted unanimously to allow us to use their building. And within a few days after this meeting, we opened up our school again. I will be eternally grateful to Senior Minister Jim Hackney and his church for their act of kindness toward our school. God worked a miracle for us as well as for them. Soon after, we were able to purchase their church property and they were able to build a new facility in a different location.

We remained in that location until our brand new school building was completed. In the fall of 2003, we opened the doors of the new Calvary Christian Academy. It is a modern day miracle. It is a state of the art, beautiful, school building equipped with the latest technology, and room enough to double the size of our enrollment. God is so faithful. We have indeed ended up with twice as much. Praise God!

We were and still are committed to the cause of Christian education. The 2004-2005 school year marked our 25th year of quality Christian education. The vision wasn't enough. It was wonderful to think about, but if our vision had not become a cause, our school would not be in operation today. It had to become a passionate cause. God has affected and changed so many lives through Calvary

Christian Academy through the years and we are excited to see what God will continue to do. The devastating storm of 2000 could not stop the cause of Christian education.

Chapter 4

IS THERE NOT A CAUSE?

*"And David said,
What have I now done?
Is there not a cause?"*
1 Samuel 17:29

As a young shepherd boy, David dreamed of great things. His big dreams far surpassed his small stature and young age. He was faithful to watch over his sheep as he had been told. No matter how small the task seemed, he continued to do what God had told him to do last. But as he tended his sheep, he dreamed of things to come. God was preparing him for his defining moment. He had already slain the lion and the bear, but his greatest victory was still to come.

"Is there not a cause?" These are the words of David in I Samuel 17:29. He arrives at the battlefield and hears the giant Philistine cursing his God. He looks at his brothers and asks them why this *"uncircumcised Philistine"* is allowed to continue to defy the armies of Israel and God

Almighty. In verse 30, David asks the question again to those around him—*"Is there not a cause?"* David does not understand why no one is willing to face the giant. But David is ready. He asks King Saul to let him fight the giant. Saul reluctantly agrees and tries to fit him with a suit of armor to protect him against the giant. But David isn't interested in the king's armor. He says, *"I have not proven this armor."* But he had proven God, who had already delivered him from the lion and the bear and this giant would be no different. He was confident because he knew the battle was the Lord's, not his own. This encounter was just what he had been waiting for all of his life. I believe every fiber of his being exploded when his purpose in life came into focus. His vision of doing great things for God had just graduated into a cause.

There were two champions on the battlefield that day. One was on his way up and one was on his way down. Goliath was about to find out the consequences of blaspheming the God of Israel, and David was about to learn the benefits of courageous obedience to a cause. David could have passed up the opportunity of a lifetime that day. His brothers passed it up and so did the rest of the Israelite army. Instead, he chose to seize the moment he was destined for. It would have been easy to pass up the opportunity because of fear or doubt. He could have just said, "That's not my problem."

The army of Israel had a great vision to win the

victory over the Philistines. They were going to be more than glad to participate in the victory celebration. The only problem was that there was a giant in the way. The victory was going to require courage and inconvenience to say the least. Obviously, it was their desire to be victorious someday, but no one except little David was willing to fight for the cause right then. You see, the vision wasn't going to accomplish the task. It was only when the vision became a cause that the giant fell. Someone was going to have to spring into action. David chose to make history that day and God used him to overcome the enemy.

> *While everyone else was simply rehearsing the problem, David made up his mind to help solve it*

David recognized that there was a problem that needed to be solved. While everyone else was simply rehearsing the problem, David made up his mind to help solve it. I believe this is a key to the importance of the cause. For example, it's one thing to lock in with the vision of your pastor and church, it's another thing to help to bring it to pass. It's one thing to recognize a problem, it's another thing to help solve it. That is the difference! David recognized the problem but he didn't stop there. He went beyond the vision of someday and embraced the cause of now.

The victory that David won over the giant that day was the defining moment in his life. It was his once-in-a-lifetime-opportunity. At first glance, the opportunity seemed to just fall into his lap. After all, David was just obediently running errands for his father when he seemingly stumbled into his cause. He was being faithful in serving others. Although it seemed like chance, it was a moment he was born for. It was a God-plan.

I remember when God first gave us the opportunity to help start a television station in Uganda, Africa. Because it seemed to spring on us suddenly, it may have appeared to some as a chance happening. But the truth is, God had been preparing us. Preparation precedes manifestation. Because of that preparation, we were able to move quickly and before we knew it, we had a 50,000 watt Christian television station that is now reaching millions with the gospel 24 hours a day, seven days a week.

We had the license. We built the studio. We contacted Trinity Broadcasting Network and they graciously agreed to provide us with invaluable help and equipment. Although we are now responsible for the daily expenses and operation of the station, we will always be grateful to

> *Preparation precedes manifestation.*

TBN for their help in the early days of Lighthouse Television.

Lighthouse Television wasn't something we were looking for. The opportunity presented itself and we moved on it. It was time to move. It may have seemed like chance, but looking back on it now, I know that God orchestrated that opportunity. We could have passed on it. We could have just decided that it was too inconvenient or costly. But I'm so thankful that we were obedient to the leading of the Spirit. Countless souls have been saved and touched by that television station. Praise God! We had always had a vision to see more souls reached with the gospel, now the cause of Lighthouse Television in Uganda, Africa is bringing it to pass.

Chapter 5

TO THIS END WAS I BORN

"…Jesus answered, Thou sayest that I am a king. To this end was I born, and for this cause came I into the world, that I should bear witness unto the truth…"
John 18:37

In John chapter 18, Jesus is on trial before Pilate, the Roman governor, just a short time before His crucifixion will occur. Pilate asks Jesus, *"Are you a King?"* I can imagine Jesus standing before the governor in the courtroom. All eyes are fixed on Him waiting eagerly for His response to the question. The response that Jesus gives has touched my heart in a way that is difficult for me to articulate. Jesus responds to the question by saying, *"To this end was I born, and for this cause came I into the world, that I should bear witness unto the truth."* In other words, Jesus was saying that this particular moment in time was why He was born. Jesus knew His cause. He knew why He was born. He came into the world to bring truth. Being before

Pilate was not a negative thing to Jesus. He could confidently stand before him and speak the truth because He had not come to save His life, but to lay it down willingly. His cause consumed Him. He was committed to His cause, even unto death on a cross.

When Jesus stood before Pilate, He had access to all of heaven's power. He had the power to eliminate all of His accusers. But He chose to cross the point of no return. Everything Jesus had accomplished up to that moment was preparation for what he was about to endure. There was no turning back. His cause had been His motivating factor. It is what brought Him to the courtroom, and it is what sustained Him throughout all of the pain and torture He suffered. Hebrews 12:2 says that it was *"for the joy that was set before Him that He endured the cross."* The momentum of His cause carried Him all the way to Calvary. He was consumed. He could do no other. It was His passion.

> *Don't quit on your first day and don't quit on your worst day.*

In John 19:30, Jesus utters the words, *"It is finished."* Jesus is a finisher. It is easy to get a vision and start something. The important thing to remember is that the starting point is not the most important point. Starting something is easy. The true sign of success will be when the job is finished. I have learned the value of the phrase "Don't quit!" I have said those words to myself and to others many, many times over the years. I have often said, "Don't quit on your first day and don't quit on your worst day." We must finish the work that God has entrusted to us. I have preached for years that it is more important to finish than to start. Imagine if David would have decided to just quit. The Israelites would have become the slaves of the Philistines. If Jesus had quit, we would be without hope. What kept them from quitting? It was the passion of the cause. Giving up is not an option. If God has called you into it, see it through. Be a finisher. Don't quit!

Chapter 6

WHAT'S IN IT FOR ME?

"What shall be done to the man that killeth this Philistine, and taketh away the reproach from Israel."
I Samuel 17:26

When I was in bible college as a young man, a profound event occurred in my life. A new girl showed up on campus. She quickly became the talk of the campus. All the guys were talking about how they were going to ask her out. They all had big plans of how they were going to approach her and win her heart. But while they were talking, I slipped out of the group and found her and did something about it. That's how I met my wife. We have now been married for fifty years. You see, those guys had a vision, *but I had a cause*. If I had waited around, I may not have received the great benefit of being married to my wife, Joy, for all of these years. My vision became a cause and I was rewarded greatly.

There are definitely benefits that come as a result of pursuing a God-given cause. God wants to reward our labor. There is something in it for you. When David stepped into his cause and defeated the giant, there were many fringe benefits. In I Samuel 17:26 David asks, *"What shall be done to the man that killeth this Philistine, and taketh away the reproach from Israel."* In other words he asked, "What's in it for me?" He was told that he would be rewarded with great riches by the king and would be given the hand of the king's daughter as well. He even got the girl! Sounds like something right out of Hollywood. The point is, knowing that there will be benefits when you pursue a cause will help keep your focus on the end goal, rather than on your present circumstances.

> *There is always excitement associated with walking in faith and the rewards are supernatural*

So much emphasis is placed upon the size of the giant in this story. However, I don't believe that David was truly focused on the giant. He had his eye on the final prize. God was getting ready to deliver the Philistine army over to the Israelites, and David was focused on the end result. He was able to see beyond the giant. Goliath was not the issue.

The cause was much greater than the giant. He was merely an obstacle in the pursuit of the cause. David had much bigger things on his mind than the giant. He could see the defeat of the Philistine army. He could see himself being rewarded with great riches and even the king's daughter. David didn't seem to be concerned about the giant at all. He wasn't even interested in trying to protect himself. He refused Saul's armor. I believe that even if Saul's armor had fit him, he would not have wanted to use it.

Why was he so confident that day when he faced the giant? Because he knew the battle was not his own. The battle was the Lord's! He was not afraid. He asked those around him, "Who does this guy think he is?" He spoke to Goliath with great confidence. He told him that he would cut off his head and feed his dead carcass to the vultures! Does this sound like he was afraid of the giant? No, the giant was not the issue. He was focused on the cause.

Another great benefit of a cause is the adventure that is associated with it. I am convinced that the reason people get involved with drugs and alcohol and other addictive behaviors is partly because they are not passionate about anything significant. They are bored. Life is dull. Somehow they have decided that drugs or alcohol bring excitement or enjoyment to their lives. When in fact, it only leads to destruction. But being passionate about a cause is an adventure. There is always excitement associated with walking in faith and the rewards are supernatural.

David's life was filled with adventure. It consisted of killing wild animals, slaying a giant, being the focus of a manhunt, becoming a king, and so many other exciting events. Of course David would not have chosen some of the events that occurred in his life, but the risk of living with a passionate cause resulted in great rewards.

Paul's cause was an exciting one as well. He was shipwrecked multiple times, lowered in a basket from a window in a wall to escape from being arrested, praised his way out of a prison cell, and so many other faith-filled adventures.

Jesus' life was also filled with excitement. There was never a dull day in his ministry. He opened blind eyes, loosed tongues, and raised the dead. He escaped death on multiple occasions. He endured the death of the cross and then came back to life again. He paid the debt of the sins and sicknesses of the world and was raised up victorious over death, hell and the grave. No one can say He lived a boring life. The point is, when you have a cause that you are willing to die for, you will never be bored.

Chapter 7

Pursuing Your Cause

"The gifts and calling of God are without repentance."
Romans 11:29

In the preceding chapters, I have attempted to highlight the differences between a vision and a cause. A vision is a great thing. It is a blueprint. It is a compass that helps guide you in the right direction. But I have also stated that at some point, the vision has to be put into action. It must graduate into a cause. Having established these things, I want this final chapter to be an encouragement to you. God has given many of you a great vision. He also wants to help you move into your cause. What is it that is burning in your heart to do? What problems do you see that you know you can help solve? These are probably indications of your cause.

It's important to note that everyone can have a cause. You do not have to be in the full-time ministry in order to have one. Regardless of your vocation, God wants you to pursue a passionate cause. If God has given you a vision for something, start taking steps toward putting it into action. That is when you will become effective. Move in the direction that your vision is pointing you. Don't despise small beginnings. God honors steps of faith.

You may be asking, "What if I have already put my vision on the shelf?" or "What if I missed my opportunity?" I have good news for you. It is not too late! I want to remind you of Romans 11:29 which says, *"The gifts and calling of God are without repentance."* God is not finished with you. He is not sorry that he has called you. He is not disappointed in you. He wants to see you burning with a passionate cause for Him. Perhaps you were passionate about a cause at an earlier time in your life, but it has now died somewhat or completely. I have good news. God is not finished with you. He is just beginning His work in you. Do not be discouraged. Your defining moment is still ahead of you.

> *God is preparing you for your defining moment.*

David's defining moment didn't take him by surprise. He was prepared for it. When it presented itself to him, he recognized what it was. God is preparing you for your defining moment. It is ahead of you. Everything that you have experienced up to this point is preparation for what God has in your future. God's best is still ahead of you. Take what you have learned in this book and let it ignite a new desire to step into your cause. Let it prepare your heart for what God is going to do in your life. Look beyond your present circumstances and see where God wants you to be, and then move in that direction. Before you know it, your vision will become a cause.

SALVATION PRAYER

- God loves us and has a wonderful plan for our lives. We can only achieve true peace and our full potential when we have a personal relationship with Him. It's sad, but most people don't achieve that peace and potential. Why?
- Because sin separates all mankind from God. The Bible says, *"All have sinned and come short of the glory of God"* (Romans 3:23). Active rebellion or passive indifference are signs of sin.
- He made provision for us through His Son Jesus. People try many different things to get to God, but Jesus is the only way we can be reunited in relationship with God. *"For there is one God, and one mediator between God and men, the man Christ Jesus"* (1 Timothy 2:5).
- God created us with a free will. We must choose to come to Him and invite Him into our lives. *"Yet to all who received Him, to those who believed in His name, He gave the right to become children of God"* (John 1:12).

If you would like that peace and union with God, simply speak to Him and mean it from your heart. Admit your need (I am a sinner). Be willing to turn away from your sins (repent). Believe that Jesus died for you on the cross and rose from the grave. Invite Jesus Christ to come in and direct your life through the Holy Spirit. (Receive Him as Lord and Savior.) You can use your own words, but here is and example:

> *Dear Lord, I am sorry for all of my sins and I want to turn away from them today, with Your help. Thank You for dying on the cross for me. I believe You rose from the dead, and are returning again – all for me. Come into my heart. Wash me, cleanse me, change me and set me free, fill me with Your Spirit and give me a hunger and passion for the things that You desire. Help me to live the full life You have for me. In Jesus' name I pray. Amen."*

If you prayed this from your heart and meant it, you have assurance form His Word, the Bible, that you are now a born-again, child of God and will spend eternity with Him. *"For whosoever shall call upon the name of the Lord shall be saved"* (Romans 10:13).

There are some important things you can do to grow in your relationship with Him. Read your Bible every day to get to know Him better. Invest time in prayer every day. Prayer is talking to God and listening to Him speak to your heart. Tell others about Him. Worship, fellowship, and serve with other Christians in a church that preaches Jesus Christ. Demonstrate your new life by love, concern and compassion for others. Welcome to the family!

If you prayed to receive Jesus Christ for the first time, please let us know. You can contact us at Calvary Cathedral International, 1701 Oakhurst Scenic Dr., Fort Worth, TX 76111. Or call us at 817.332.1246. We'd love to hear from you!

Calvary Cathedral International Prayer Ministry

The Power Tower is the 24-hour prayer ministry of Calvary Cathedral International. Since May of 1995 we have been praying 24 hours a day, 7 days a week for our church, our nation and the world. Trained prayer leaders and pray-ers praying in 2-hour shifts receive prayer requests by telephone, fax, e-mail and via our web site.

We are on way to receiving over 500,000 prayer requests from across the United States and around the world.

God hears and answers prayer as we receive reports of amazing answers to prayer of how people are healed of terminal illnesses, families and marriages are restored, financial breakthroughs are manifested, and most important of all, people are being saved.

If you need prayer, you can call us at 817.332.4284. Your request will be prayed over every two hours for the next 24 hours.

Calvary Cathedral International Bible School

Calvary Cathedral International Bible School is designed to help believers mature in the things of God by learning His Word in an atmosphere of faith and love. The Bible School curriculum gives students Biblical knowledge and teaches who you are and what you have in Christ. It helps you develop the fruit of the Spirit in your life as you discover your gifts and calling by submitting yourself to His Word and serving God. At Calvary Cathedral International Bible School, you will establish life-long friendships with other students as you learn His Word. CCIBS is recognized by the Veteran's Administration for qualified veterans. CCIBS has approval by the Immigration and Naturalization Service for qualified foreign students.

The first week of classes is open without charge for anyone who is interested in visiting before making a decision. For further information, please call our office at 817.332.1246.

For other ministry products by Pastor Bob Nichols, contact the Calvary Cathedral International Bookstore by phone at 817.332.3736, or by e-mail at backley@calvarycathedral.org.

Written correspondence should be sent to:
Calvary Cathedral International Bookstore
1701 Oakhurst Scenic Drive
Fort Worth, Texas 76111

Notes

Notes